MY FIRST
BOOK OF
PRAYERS

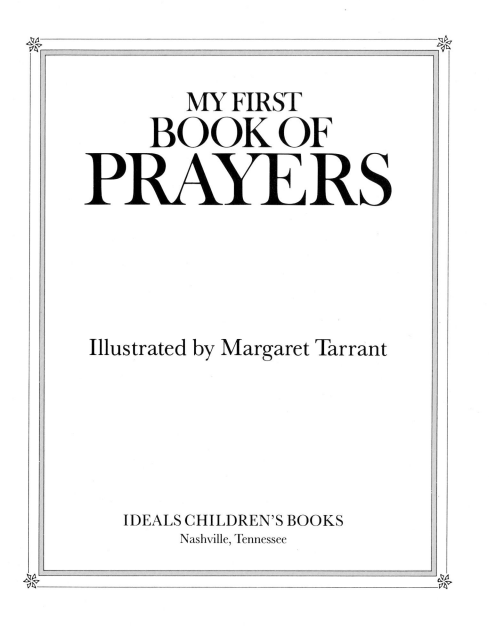

MY FIRST
BOOK OF
PRAYERS

Illustrated by Margaret Tarrant

IDEALS CHILDREN'S BOOKS
Nashville, Tennessee

GRACE

Thank you for the food we eat,
Thank you for the flowers so sweet,
Thank you for the birds that sing,
Thank you God, for everything.

Amen

OUR BEAUTIFUL WORLD

Heavenly Father, this is a beautiful world.
Thank you for mountains and rivers,
hills and valleys, forests and fields,
and for all the wonderful beauty of nature.
Please help us to care for
the lovely planet you have given us.

Amen

THE LORD'S PRAYER

Our Father, who art in heaven,
Hallowed be thy name;
Thy kingdom come,
Thy will be done, on earth as it is in heaven.
Give us this day our daily bread;
And forgive us our trespasses,
As we forgive those that trespass against us;
And lead us not into temptation,
But deliver us from evil.
For thine is the kingdom,
the power and the glory,
For ever and ever.

Amen

FOR FLOWERS AND PLANTS

Dear God, thank you for creating flowers.
It is wonderful to watch them grow
from tiny seeds,
to see them open and to smell them.
Thank you for all plants that grow; they make
our world a beautiful place.

Amen

THANK YOU FOR TAKING CARE OF ME

Dear Jesus,
I know that you are with me all the time,
watching over me and keeping me safe.
Thank you for all the care you take of me
and of all children everywhere.

Amen

SHARING

Help me to share in all I do,
Whether at home or play or school.
Help me to join in all the fun,
Never to be the only one
Who's angry and grumpy and all alone.
Help me to smile and not to moan.
For in the world there will always be
Others who aren't as lucky as me.

Amen

FOR BOOKS

Heavenly Father, thank you for books:
story books, books that make us laugh or cry,
books that we make ourselves to keep
special pictures and cards in,
and books that help us to understand
the world about us.
Thank you for the gift of reading
and all the pleasure it brings.

Amen

FOR BIRDS

Dear Lord,
For all the birds that sing and fly
And soar across the great, blue sky,
From giant eagle to tiny wren,
We thank you very much.

Amen

BUBBLES

Dear Jesus, thank you for all the little things
that make life so much fun.

Amen

FOR WINDY DAYS

For windy days when I love to run and shout,
Thank you.
For all the winds that roar around the Earth,
Thank you.
For kites that jump and sail in the air and
give us so much fun,
Thank you.

Amen

FOR CHILDREN
WHO ARE ILL

Dear Jesus, I pray for all children who are ill.
Help them to be brave and patient and to get
better quickly.
Please also help all the people who look after
us when we are ill,
especially doctors and nurses.

Thank you for the gift of good health.

Amen

IN MY SMALL CORNER

Dear God, when I look at all the stars and
planets in the sky,
remind me that, even though the Earth where
I live is only a tiny part of the
Universe which you made, you watch over
me in my small corner
and care for me every day.

Amen

WHEN I'M SHY

Dear Jesus, when I feel shy and don't want to
join in, help me to be brave
and friendly like you. And when other people
are shy, help me to remember
what it feels like and to be friendly to them.

Amen

FOR WATER

Dear Lord, thank you for streams and ponds,
lakes and rivers. They give us beautiful places
to play and water to drink. There are many
places in the world where people do not have
enough water to drink or to grow their food.
Please help us to help them.

Amen

FOR FRIENDS

Dear Jesus, friend of all children, thank you
for my friends.
When they are sad, help me to make them
happier.
When they are frightened, help me to make
them brave.
When no one likes them, help me to stand by
them.
Help us always to play happily together and
make me a good friend to have.

Amen

FOR PICTURES

Thank you, dear Lord, for eyes to see and
hands to paint and draw.
Thank you, too, for all artists who paint and
draw pictures. I like looking at pictures: they
show me the beauty and wonders of our
world.
Teach me to use my eyes and hands so
that I can show others your creation.

Amen

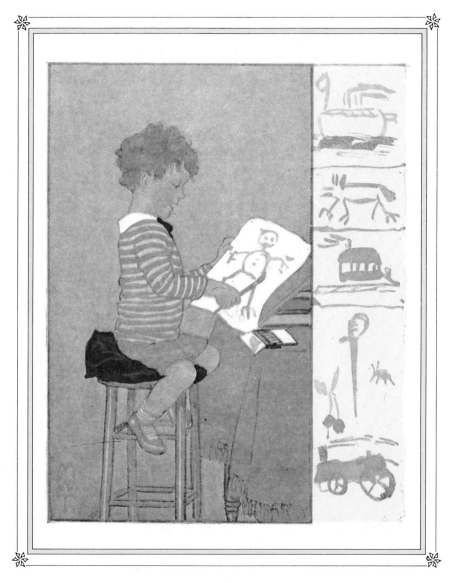

FOR HEALTH AND STRENGTH

Thank you, Lord, for strength to run and
jump and play.
Please care for all those children who are ill or
handicapped.
Make them strong and healthy so that they
can enjoy themselves as I do.

Amen

ALL THINGS
BRIGHT AND BEAUTIFUL

All things bright and beautiful,
All creatures great and small,
All things wise and wonderful,
The Lord God made them all.

He gave us eyes to see them,
And lips that we might tell
How great is God Almighty,
Who has made all things well.

Amen

THE SPRING

Dear God, when spring comes flowers open,
birds sing, animals wake,
and I can play outside again.
Thank you for creating such a beautiful time
of year.

Amen

FOR THE SUN

For the sun which shines on us,
Thank you God.
For the warmth and light it gives,
Thank you God.
For the sun that makes everything grow,
Thank you God.

Amen

FOR SNOW

Dear God, you make every snowflake that
falls a wonderful new pattern.
Thank you for snow that makes city streets
beautiful and gives us so much fun.

Amen

FOR ALL CHILDREN, EVERYWHERE

Heavenly Father, you made us all,
The rich and poor, great and small.
All the children beneath the sun,
You care for every single one.
Help me to love all the rest,
Whether from North, South, East or West.
Wherever we live, we know that we
Are all part of God's family.

Amen

PETS

Dear Lord, thank you for pets that keep us
company and share our lives.
Help me always to be kind to animals and
look after them properly. Help me to
remember to feed them and not to leave their
cages for someone else to clean.

Amen

WHEN I'M NOT VERY NICE TO KNOW

Sometimes I say unkind things which hurt
other people.
Sometimes I am very unfriendly.
Sometimes I quarrel, even with my best
friend.
Sometimes I do things which I know I
shouldn't do.

Dear Lord, I'm sorry for all the things that
I've done wrong. Please forgive me and help
me to be kind and loving.

Amen

51

FOR ANIMALS

Dear God,
You made all creatures great and small,
The elephants, the lions, and giraffes so tall,
The hissing snakes, and insects that crawl.
Help me to care for them and protect them all.

Amen

FOR THE SEASIDE

Dear Jesus,

For feeling sand beneath my feet,
For many friends that I will meet,
For all the sun's great light and heat,
I thank you.

For sandcastles as big as mountains,
For waves to jump and splash about in,
For helping me to learn to swim,
I thank you.

Amen

MY HOME

Heavenly Father, thank you for my home and my family, and for all the grown-ups who look after me.

Please care for all the children in the world who do not have someone to look after them or a home to live in. Please give them the love and shelter that they need and keep them safe from harm.

Amen

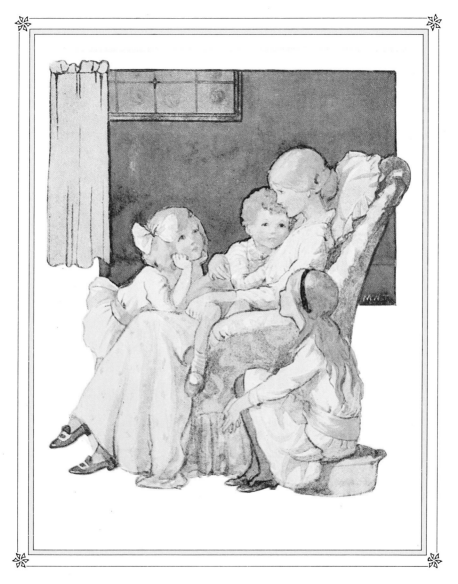

FOR THE SEA

For seas that swirl around the Earth and all
The creatures that live in them:
Seals that swim in cold waters,
Sharks that hunt in the deep,
Whales that cross oceans,
Fish, crabs, corals, and shells,
We thank you Lord.

Amen

CHRISTMAS

Dear God, when we are having lots of fun at Christmas, help us to remember that your son Jesus was born to save us all. Thank you for the gift of his life.

Amen

EVENING HYMN

Now the day is over,
Night is drawing nigh,
Shadows of the evening
Steal across the sky.

Now the darkness gathers,
Stars begin to peep,
Birds and beasts and flowers
Soon will be asleep.

Through the long night watches
May your angels spread
Their white wings above me,
Watching round my bed.

When the morning wakens,
Then may I arise
Pure and fresh and sinless
In your holy eyes.

S. Baring-Gould 1834-1924